Command Your

Money

Powerful Keys to Provoke Financial

Breakthrough

DANIEL C. OKPARA

Published By:

Better Life Media.

BETTER LIFE WORLD OUTREACH CENTER.

Website: www.BetterLifeWorld.org

Email: info@betterlifeworld.org

FOLLOW US ON FACEBOOK

1. **Like our Page on Facebook** for updates

2. **Join Our Facebook Prayer Group**, submit prayer requests and follow powerful daily prayers for total victory and breakthrough

This title and others are available for quantity discounts for sale promotions, gifts, and evangelism. Visit our website or email us to get started.

Any scripture quotation used in this book is taken from the New King James Version, except where stated. Used by permission.

Table of Contents

RECEIVE DAILY AND WEEKLY PRAYERS

Powerful Prayers Sent to Your Inbox Every Monday

Enter your email address to receive notifications of new posts, prayers and prophetic declarations sent to you by email.

Email Address

Sign Me Up

Go to: **BreakThroughPrayers.org** to subscribe to receive FREE WEEKLY PRAYER POINTS, and prophetic declarations sent to you by email.

FREE BOOKS ...

Download These 4 Powerful Books Today for FREE...
Take Your Relationship With God to a New Level.

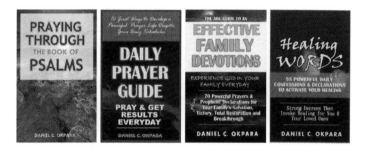

Go Here to Download: www.betterlifeworld.org/grow

Introduction

Are you currently embroiled in a financial situation?

Do you need a breakthrough asap?

Are you looking for a simple-to-follow instruction that will trigger a financial breakthrough for you very quickly?

Then get home tonight, close your door and begin to apply these spiritual instructions, and you'll see miracles happen in your finances. More importantly, you'll have the wisdom to move forward financially.

This is a no-fluff, no long stories, practical, and provoking Biblical instructions for dealing with urgent money problems

I've sat and prayed with more people needing help financially than any other area. At first, I thought it was because of my environment. However, with the growth of my evangelism and prayer blog, www.betterlifeworld.org, the experience is looking the same.

About sixty out of a hundred of the prayer requests I receive on the blog (and I get quite a good number of them every day) dwells on finance. The details are usually different, but when summarized, they boil down to money - Money to pay bills, money to get a new house, money to invest on something, failing business, debtors not wanting to pay, grace for debt cancellation, contract to be approved, money to support health treatment, grace for recovery of lost investments, urgent need for better job, etc.

It's more startling because ninety percent of these blog readers and prayer requesters are not from Africa. Majority of my (over 9,500) subscribers are from nations that make up the successful world. So my initial thought that most of these money problems were environmental is wrong. Money problem is a universal problem. While the details may differ, the generalities are the same.

So if money is such an important issue in our daily lives, why are we not giving time to discuss it practically in the church today?

Oh, I know. The world doesn't want us to talk about money. They have a set of things they want the church to teach, and money is not part of it. Fortunately, if there is a place people should have balanced, in-depth teaching about the subject of money, it should be in the church.

If we only talk about money when we want to raise an offering, that's unfair. Jesus talked about money and possessions several times, often using parables (sixteen of them) to show us what our attitude should be on money matters. He taught on greed, priority, hard work, profit-making, employer-employee relationship, and so on. He gave a balanced teaching on money and possessions, and so should we.

What most Christians know about money today stops at giving and seed-sowing. Unfortunately, they've sowed and sowed and haven't prospered as they learned. The reason is simple: Money giving will not invoke God's blessings when other variables are missing.

In this book, I am focusing more on these missing variables that can delay a person's financial blessings. These teachings were initially my *sermon notes on breaking financial hardship,* and it still is. I believe that the instructions contained in these pages will empower you to command financial breakthrough as soon as possible.

To be clear, this is not a book on financial management or business opportunities. I have drawn from the spiritual insights that God gave me during prayer and study about solving financial hardship. A few points may interface with issues you'll see in regular business and finance books. Where this happens, know that those truths have their roots in the Scriptures, and have personally helped me in real life - in understanding the psychology of money.

I believe that God will speak to your heart as you turn these pages and you will command your financial breakthrough in the shortest possible time, in Jesus name.

Amen.

Action #1: **Start Declaring the Word**

"He sent His word and healed them, and delivered them from their destructions." - Psalm 107:20

One of the areas that Christians are facing a lot of battles today is in the area of their finances. The devil knows that **money in the hand of a Christian is an instrument of warfare**. With money, a Christian is empowered to take his world, his environment, and his community for Christ. This is one of the reasons the devil fights believers' finances more than anything else.

While I agree that there are many reasons people could be suffering from financial hardship, the word of God is clear that God does not delight in the economic woes of His children. It is not the will of God for you to be unable to pay your children's school fees; it is not His will for you to always have to beg to meet your financial obligations.

> Let them shout for joy and rejoice, who favor my vindication and want what is right for me; Let them say continually, *"Let the Lord be*

magnified, who delights and takes pleasure in the prosperity of His servant." - Psalm 35:27 (AMP)

God delights in your prosperity. That is, He takes pleasure in your financial wellbeing.

You may be going through a rough situation at the moment, but don't let that make you forget the will of God for your life and finances. Continually repeat to yourself that God delights in your prosperity, not in your lack. That's how to get started.

Our Warfare is Real

The scripture is clear that we are in warfare (See Rev. 12:7-11 & Ephesians 6:12). If you still think that this battle is a child's play, you better wake up.

There is a severe spiritual conflict going on against humanity, against your life, against your home, against your marriage, and against your finances. The devil is doing all he can to create all manner of obstructions and restrictions that will eventually keep you far from God's promises. His goal is to get you to the point of doubt and total discouragement. Don't let him.

I love the way a friend of mine, Pastor Samuel Israel, echoed it. He said, *"Financial breakthrough is spiritual warfare."*

He's right.

So what are your first steps to winning this war over your finances?

1. Keep Standing and Keep Serving

When you're going through financial problems, it's easy to feel so overwhelmed with the situation that you get off from God if you're not watchful. The devil might begin to plant thoughts in your mind that makes you think that the Word of God is not working. He might send people who will discourage you from spiritual things. You may have opportunities to quit church and remember how the church didn't help you in your situation.

Sometimes, the devil can get you so busy with running up and down looking for a financial way out that you don't have time to attend services or listen to God's word again. He may even make you feel that pastors are part of your problem.

But don't let the devil succeed with that.

Don't let the devil succeed with starving you of God's Word when you're going through intense situations, including financial challenges. Spiritual starvation is the recipe for total collapse and disaster.

I've seen people who get offended with their church because the church did not assist them in their crisis. They stopped going to church for many years. Unfortunately, their situations didn't get better.

During times of crisis of any kind, that is the time to go deeper in the things of God. Refuse the temptation of getting offended by the attitudes of people. Strive to be focused on Jesus and His WORD. Go deeper. Go deeper. Go deeper.

Beware of spiritual starvation when facing financial problems

According to Hebrews 12:1-2, *"...Since we are surrounded by so great a cloud of witnesses, let us lay aside every weight and the sin which so easily ensnares us, and let us run with endurance the race that is set before us. Looking unto Jesus, the author and finisher of our faith, who for the joy that was set before Him endured the cross, despising the shame, and has sat down at the right hand of the throne of God."*

There are times that we have to put up with the hostility of people and endure some hardship while waiting and letting God work on our faith and expectations. It's all part of the process of our faith, service, and manifesting His promises.

I know you'll say, "But I desperately need help. I can't endure anymore."

I know. But stay with God. It's His help that will set you free.

2. Stop Complaining; Start Commanding

Moving forward from serving and standing, you need to arm yourself with God's Word on finances. God's Word is His will. Find His promises, read them, assure yourself of them, and begin to declare the promises.

Stop complaining, stop begging, and stop declaring how terrible things are. Start claiming God's promises for your welfare and prosperity. His promises will release His grace for every situation and command breakthrough.

"Pastor, you won't understand," you say. "I'm in a very tight corner right now. I need money urgently. The bills are overdue. I don't want to lose my home."

I understand.

But I'm showing you the practical way forward.

> ***Your situation is a fact, but God's Word is the solution.***

What to Do Now

What is God saying about your finances?

Open your Bible; begin to locate scriptures on God's plan for your provision and finances. Go back to these promises you've heard, read them again and again; read them out in the middle of the night for many days, internalize them, mutter them, sleep on them, speak them, and fight with them. That's the first step to command your money and release your breakthrough.

Heaven and earth will pass away. Those things mocking you today will surely pass away. But the Word of God will never fall to the ground.

Action #2: **16 Powerful Declarations to Reprogram Yourself for Supernatural Breakthrough**

₈But what saith it? The word is nigh thee, even in thy mouth, and in thy heart: that is, the word of faith, which we preach;

₉That if thou shalt confess with thy mouth the Lord Jesus, and shalt believe in thine heart that God hath raised him from the dead, thou shalt be saved. ₁₀For with the heart man believeth unto righteousness, and with the mouth confession is made unto salvation. – Rom. 10:8-10

Below are confessions based on God's promises for your provision and financial prosperity. Internalize these scripture-composed declarations and make them your daily and nightly affirmations going forward. Wake up in the middle of the night and read the corresponding verses and declare the assertions out loud. Declare them early in the morning, mid-day, evening, and every time you can.

Find other scriptures and add to the examples presented here, and go to war with them. The Word of God is the

Sword of the Spirit. As you release these scriptures from your mouth, you're releasing missiles in the spirit realm to deal with every satanic obstacle against your life and finances. You're releasing grace for your breakthrough.

Don't just think on these scriptures. Speak them out, shout them, and declare them out of your mouth. Turn their messages into scripture warfare.

> ***Refuse to allow the enemy to steal your finances or obstruct your breakthrough from now onwards. Enough is enough.***

These first steps are essential. Don't ignore them and rush down to other chapters looking for money-making ideas. The spiritual controls the physical. Once you command spiritual breakthrough, you'll experience physical breakthrough.

1. Money Will Serve Me

"I reject the god called mammon. I reject greed and love of money in my heart. I ask God for mercy in every area of my life that I have exhibited greed, self-indulgence, and insatiability. I receive grace for contentment, while

I aspire to reach greater heights in God's purpose for my life.

Money is meant to serve me and not me to serve it.

I will not put money ahead of integrity, no matter what. As I seek and serve God, He will continue to supply all my needs, in Jesus name."

- (Matthew 6:24, 1 Timothy 6:10, Hebrews 13:5)

2. God Will Supply My Needs

"God will supply my needs according to His riches in glory in Jesus Christ, not according to my bank balance. I, therefore, renew my trust in God and decree that I am not afraid of whatever happens. As the following needs below are staring at me right now **(mention those specific needs)***, I confess that I am confident that God is in control and will meet these needs on time, in Jesus name"* (Philippians 4:19)

3. I Am Abounding in Grace for Good Works

"The real purpose of money and God's provisions is for me to abound in good works. I am created to be a blessing to others. God is able to make all grace abound to me, so that having all sufficiency in all things at all

times, I may abound in every good work, in Jesus name." (2 Corinthians 9:8)

4. If God Cares for Birds, Certainly, He Cares for Me

"The birds of the air do not sow nor reap nor gather into barns. They do not have bank accounts; they do not save, invest, buy and sell. Yet God feeds them and takes care of them. And I am more valuable than them.

If God does take care of these birds and other animals that do not even work, I am very confident that He will take care of me and my family at all times, and in all situations, in Jesus name." (Matthew 6:26, Job 38:41)

5. I Refuse to Let Worry and Anxiety Rule My Life

I am not going to be like the people of the world who worry and fight for houses, clothes, food, and drinks. I am a child of God through Christ Jesus. I am saved and going to heaven. While I live in this world, God knows all my needs. And he will provide for me as I continue to serve Him, put Him first in my life, and strive daily to live as He wants me to, in Jesus name." (Matthew 6:31-32)

6. God is Leading Me to My Green Pastures

Through the Holy Spirit, the Lord is my Shepherd; He is providing everything I need! As His sheep, He is leading me and bringing me to green pastures where I will lay down in abundance.

He leads me beside the quiet waters and renews my strength every day.

He empowers me to live and walk in righteousness and do what pleases Him on a daily basis. Even when I'm going through very tough times, I will not let fear rule my heart, for God is with me. He is protecting and guiding me all through the situation.

God is preparing a table for me, and I will enjoy, even in the presence of my enemies. He is anointing my head with oil, and my cup will run over.

God's goodness and unfailing kindness shall be with me all of my life, and afterward, I will live with Him forever in heaven, in Jesus name." – (Psalm 23:1-6)

7. I Will Remain Thankful

Once again, I declare that I will not be anxious about anything. Yes, sometimes my heart may be afraid, and the situation before me may look hopeless and critical. But, in everything, I reject fear and worry. I am thankful to God in all, and I'm convinced that He will never leave me nor forsake me. His plans for me are plans for peace and not of evil.

It doesn't matter what's happening today; I am very very confident that God is bringing me to the future He plans for me, a great and prosperous one, in the name of Jesus Christ. (Jeremiah 29:11, Philippians 4:6)

8. My Seeds of Faith and Righteousness Will Produce

"Dear Heavenly Father, I have sowed a lot of seeds many times as You provided for me. I acknowledge, Lord, that there have been times when I gave with a wrong mindset, and even planted in places that were not good grounds. In those times, Lord, I ask for Your mercy and forgiveness.

O Lord, You are the One who supplies seed to the sower and bread for food to the eater. I pray, Lord, multiply my seeds and increase the harvest of my righteousness in Christ Jesus. Enrich me in every way so that I will be generous in every way, and produce thanksgiving to You at all times, in Jesus name." (2 Corinthians 9:8-11)

9. I Have All Things That Apply to Life

"I decree today that God's divine power has granted to me all things that pertain to life and godliness, for He has called me unto glory and excellence. Through knowledge provided by the Holy Spirit, I will access every blessing that God has ordained for me, in Jesus name" (2 Peter 1:3

10. God is a Good Father

"Physical parents, though human and full of evil, desires good things for their children and provide for them according to their power. How much more God, our heavenly Father.

I decree today that as I ask, seek and knock, I shall receive, and find, and the door shall be opened unto me. I will receive all the good things that I desire and have asked of the Lord. I will not be embarrassed or put to shame because of money, for God owns all the money on this earth, in the name of Jesus Christ." (Matthew 7:7-11)

11. God will Never Forsake Me

"God does not forsake those who serve and trust Him.

I am a child of God, and my trust is in Him. He will never forsake me, no matter what. I will never beg bread to eat because He will always empower me to have abundance in all things, and at all times, in Jesus name." (Psalm 37:25)

12. I Will Never Lack Any Good Thing

"The young lions may suffer want and hunger, but those who seek the Lord lack no good thing. I, therefore, lack no good thing, in Jesus name." (Psalm 34:10)

13. I Will Not Labor in Vain

"I shall eat the labor of my hands, and it shall be well with me, in Jesus name" (Psalms 128:2)

14. My Prosperity is God's Will

"I will prosper and be in good health, even as my soul is flourishing, for my prosperity is God's will." – (3 John 1:2)

15. I Have the Power to Create Wealth

"Wealth creation is part of the covenant. I am a seed of Abraham through Jesus Christ. I am connected to His blessing. God has empowered me to create wealth. It doesn't matter where I am today; I am creating

generational wealth. I am an employer of labor, in Jesus name." – (Deut. 8:18)

16. I Shall Be Blessed on All Sides

"I have set my heart to walk in obedience to God's Word. I am therefore free from the curses of disobedience.

I shall be blessed in the city and blessed in the field. The fruit of my body and the fruit of my ground shall be blessed. I will increase on every side.

My going out and coming in shall be blessed. Those who rise against me in one way shall scatter in seven directions. My investments and efforts shall be blessed. The Lord shall establish me for Himself, and all the people of the earth shall know that I am called of the Lord.

God will make me plenteous in goods, in the fruit of my body, and in the fruit of my cattle, and in the fruit of my ground, in the land which the LORD has located me. The windows of heaven are open unto me. There shall be rain in my land in season. The works of my hand shall be blessed. I shall be the head only and not the tail. I shall lend unto nations, and shall not borrow.

In the name of Jesus Christ" – (Deut. 28:1-14)

Action #3: **10 Things You Can Do Right Now to Deal With Urgent Financial Situations**

It was 2:00 am. My phone rang. I should have been asleep, but because I was writing, I picked up.

"Hello, Brother...How are you?" I asked.

"I'm stressed out Pastor. I need an urgent financial breakthrough."

He was straight to the point. No painting the situation

"Ok," I replied. "Talk to me. What's happening?"

For the next ten minutes, he reeled out what appeared to be an intense situation. "I've been praying, confessing sins, praising, and doing everything I know how to do, but...I need help. I need prayers please," he concluded.

"Wow," I empathized. "This must be very hard right now."

After asking a few questions, I said, "Can we read the Bible?"

"Sure," he replied.

"Ok," I said. "Get me the book of 2Kings 4: 1-7. Read it out and share your lessons with me."

As we read those verses and talked, I could see that he got the lessons.

You see, when we are in a financial situation, we're often not in the right frame of mind. But if we can subject ourselves to the Scriptures, other than just praying, we'll be able to ask ourselves the right questions and obtain the correct answers as quickly as possible.

Let me share with you important things you can do if you find yourself in a financial situation. These instructions will work no matter what the problem is because God's Word will always produce. They are the same keys from 2Kings chapter 4 that I discussed with my early morning caller. Let's read verse 1-7:

> ₁A certain woman of the wives of the sons of the prophets cried out to Elisha, saying, "Your servant my husband is dead, and you know that your servant feared the Lord. And the creditor is coming to take my two sons to be his slaves."

₂ So Elisha said to her, **"What shall I do for you? Tell me, what do you have in the house?"** And she said, *"Your maidservant has nothing in the house but a jar of oil."*

₃ Then he said, "Go, borrow vessels from everywhere, from all your neighbors—empty vessels; do not gather just a few. ₄ And when you have come in, you shall shut the door behind you and your sons; then pour it into all those vessels, and set aside the full ones."

₅ So she went from him and shut the door behind her and her sons, who brought the vessels to her; and she poured it out. ₆ Now it came to pass, when the vessels were full, that she said to her son, "Bring me another vessel."

And he said to her, "There is not another vessel." So the oil ceased. ₇ Then she came and told the man of God. And he said, "Go, sell the oil and pay your debt; and you and your sons live on the rest."

This story contains powerful divine ideas for handling critical financial situations. These provoking ideas will help you resolve any financial situation that you are currently going through.

1. Balance Spirituality With Responsibility

In this story, the dead husband of this widow was referred to as a good man who feared and revered the Lord. He was a true prophet of God. He is what you would call today, a holiness preacher, or a very seriously committed believer. I believe that his prayer and worship life was exemplary and he was indeed a faithful follower of God.

Unfortunately, he died in debt. He was a true prophet, a holy man of God who learned to follow God, but sadly, never learned how to use his faith to solve his financial problems. We don't know how he died, whether he was sick or not. But I believe he must have prayed for some miraculous breakthrough and never got it.

In fact, I believe that this prophet died out of frustration. The posture of his creditors even after he was dead will give you a glimpse of the things they must have done to him while he was alive. These guys (the creditors) came for his two children when he was dead. That's a dire situation.

Notice that God did not kill these creditors even though this was the Old Testament times. So don't think He will kill your creditors today because you are praying *die by fire* prayers. You'd be better off learning God's wisdom for financial blessings.

But the question is, where did this servant of God miss it and what can we learn from him?

First, spirituality is not an antidote to poverty and lack. You can be very spiritual and still be suffering from financial problems. We have a lot of very spiritual Christians today who are suffering from all manner of financial crisis. It is not because God hates them or that they are living in secret sins, but because they have developed their spiritual lives without developing their financial lives as well.

Holiness, prophesying, speaking in tongues, and other spiritual exercises do not invoke money to solve your money problems. Everything in life is not about prayer, fasting, and spirituality. You need wisdom for financial abundance to excel financially.

In other words, **you can be so prayerful, and still be suffer-full if you don't know what you're supposed to do about money, or if you leave it all up to God to do them for you.**

The point is this: *Develop your financial knowledge as you're developing your spiritual awareness.* If you don't, life will always bounce back at you with lack, scarcity and financial crisis.

God is not the one who caused the problem this prophet found himself. I can tell you boldly that it wasn't God who killed that prophet. It wasn't Him who made him miserable, and He wasn't also using His situation to test him. God does not test you with financial crisis.

Almost all the time that people experience a financial crisis, if you check well, they led themselves to where they found themselves. Yes, I've talked about the need to pray and declare the sieges of the enemy over. But there's need for a balance. You must learn to take responsibility for your financial mistakes and not act as if God was the one who brought you there.

God is not the one who told you to skip paying your mortgage and use the money for shopping. He is not the one who told you to live in a house that you can't afford just because you feel that's the kind of home you should live in. He is not the one who told you to invest in that get-rich-quick scheme where you lost money. He is not the one who told you to send your children to that costly private school, and now you are finding it difficult to pay school fees. He is not the one who told you to go and borrow money.

Yes, God wants to help you. But first things first. Take responsibility while seeking God's help and mercy. And understand that financial breakthrough is beyond prayer, fasting, and spirituality. While praying and decreeing God's Word into the spirit realm, there are other things one must do...Begin to develop your financial knowledge.

2. Don't Die in Silence

Another lesson to learn from this story that will help you as quickly as possible is this: Cry out for help. You don't know it all.

The dead prophet refused to speak out. He could have gone to Elisha and received Elisha's ministry, but he probably thought it wasn't necessary. He stuck to praying and fasting and died out of frustration.

Thank God that his wife refused to let what killed the husband to kill her. She cried out. She sought help from those who knew more than her.

There are times that a preacher needs the ministry of other preachers. No one knows it all. When you see a particular grace in someone else's life, go for it. Don't get stuck fasting and praying and crying all night. Simple counseling or declaration from this person can resolve what years of fasting and praying may not do.

"What if they are unreachable?" You ask. It's possible. In that case, find ways to get connected to their grace. Listen to their messages, read their books, and sow into their lives, even from a distance. God who sees in the secret will reward you openly.

I say again...

> ***Don't die in silence when you're in an intense situation. Cry out for help.***

Open up and receive guidance and counseling from those who are ahead of you and can help you. It's not by age; it's by grace.

What you need is in the hand of someone else. If you don't step out and make moves, you'll die where you are. Get up from your prayers and begin to ask, "What can I do from here?"

Go and pick up a few books and begin to look for answers. Start making calls and ask what you can do.

"What if I'm misunderstood and rejected?" Well, it's part of the entire process. "A rejection is nothing more than a necessary step in the pursuit of success," says Bo Bennett. Be prepared that people will misunderstand you the moment you begin to take steps to ask for the help you need. But don't forget this: If where you are now is not where you want to be, then, other than praying and fasting, you must do something about it.

3. Choose *the Right* Over *the Convenient*

Actions of today do not end today. What you're doing today will affect your children tomorrow. Always think about that when trying to make money decisions.

Even though you need money urgently, don't go for everything that is convenient. Go for what is right. The prophet in our story went for what was convenient. He borrowed without thinking about the broader consequences. Unfortunately, it killed him. And even in death, his children were not spared.

There's one thing you can be very sure of: The troubles you're going through today will undoubtedly come to pass. But your words, decisions, and actions will be remembered for a long time to come. Strive to make it a good remembrance. Don't forget: *"Better is a little with righteousness than vast revenues without justice"* (Prov. 16:8).

4. Discern the Oil in Your House

Go back and reread our reference story. There was always a pot of oil in the house of this man of God. This oil could have saved him, but he didn't know it.

The same applies to most of us today. When we are going through financial situations, we often look away from ourselves and want some sky shaking things to happen. We begin to wish to receive a call from someone saying that God told them to give us some money. While that may happen a few times, we can't live our lives waiting for such miracles only. We need to look inward and see what we have that God will use.

Always remember this:

> ***God will not use what you don't have. He will only use what you have to create what you need.***

And the good news is that everyone has something. You may think you don't have something that can help you out of your present situation, but you do. That's your pot of oil. You have to prayerfully find it.

For some people, their pot of oil is their skill. For some others, it is their experience. While for some it is their connections. But everyone has something.

A young man came to me for prayers and counseling for financial breakthrough. After prayers, I asked, "What do you do?" When he told me what he does, I realized that he needed to learn internet ways to market this skill and he would never have to beg for money again.

Many of us are busy chasing what we don't have, believing that our financial breakthrough and success lies in those things. Unfortunately, that is not true. There is something everyone has that they can use to begin immediately to deal with the financial problems.

I want to challenge you today to discover what you have that you're not using, something that is meant to create what you want. God has blessed us all with gifts, skills, opportunities and open doors for success. Go home and lock yourself in the room today and begin to ask yourself what your pot of oil is.

We may not all be graced the same way, but we're all graced. Find your grace and grow it.

5. Borrow for *Profit,* Not for *Survival*

I had an experience when I was getting married. Someone realized that when I receive a budget for something, I would cut it and say, "This is the amount I have for that." If they gave me a food budget of 200,000 (about $700), I would say, "Okay, I have 80, 000 (about $250)." It was getting on the nerves of the different families helping to organize the wedding. So this wonderful person offered to give me a loan. "You can pay me after the wedding," he said.

But after careful thought and prayers, I refused and said, "I will do what I can and leave the rest. Thank God the date for the wedding is set already. I'm sure that day will come and pass. We will not die."

I was right. The date came and passed. I exchanged vows with my wife. Those who felt I didn't spend enough money can go ahead and do theirs. I did what I could afford.

I have long learned that borrowing is only permissible if it is for profit and not for survival. If I take a loan and get married, I might need loans to stay married.

Unfortunately, that's what many people do today. They are living their lives to impress others. So they don't mind getting some loans here and there to get some things going. Sadly, living off loans and debt is a horrible economic lifestyle.

In our reference story above, this prophet likely borrowed to pay bills or do some shopping. That's likely what happened because if he borrowed for business and the business failed, the Bible would have said so.

Now notice that this prophet in our story borrowed and landed in financial crisis. That's what borrowing can cause when it is for anything other than profit creation. But the wife borrowed, and business was created. The difference is the purpose for which the borrowed asset served.

Wait. Don't rush off and say, "Hey, pastor, that woman borrowed to finance her oil business, I think I need to look for where I can borrow too. I need some cash to push an idea right now."

While borrowing intended to create profit is better, compared to borrowing to service bills, the borrowing in this story is not a money borrowing. The vessels that the woman borrowed can be likened to renting of materials, resource persons, and or skills that one does not have, for the purpose of creating some instant profit.

So yes, if there are some skills or other materials that you need to complement what you can quickly do to market your pot of oil, you can rent these skills or materials and negotiate with the providers. The point is for you to find out what you can do as quickly as possible when you're in a financial crisis. Identify what you need to get those things ready for the market. Borrow what you don't have that is required.

"How about borrowing money?" You ask.

Well, if you're going to borrow to multiply the oil in your house and sell, that's okay. That is, borrowing to push a business.

There are times that we may need additional capital to get some things going. Provided it is intended to create profit, borrowing is permissible. But the narrative must be clear enough that the loan is designed to support something that will generate profit. This is because when you're in a financial predicament, it is not always the best time to borrow money, because it may lead to further crisis.

6. Shut Your Door

The next instruction Elisha gave this woman after the direction to borrow is to shut the door. What does this mean?

Close your ears from people's opinions and gossips.

If you're going to come out of any financial predicament, you must block your ears from listening to people's doubts, fears and expectations of you. Do not let what people will say stop you from taking small-step actions of faith. Do not let them stop you from doing small things. If you succeed tomorrow, they will come back to ask for help.

There are times that to be back up financially, you need to start in the smallest of endeavors. The biggest challenge you will have is comparing with your past and then saying that you're too big for something.

No one is too big for anything. As a matter of fact, if you feel too big to do small things, then you're too small to do big things. If you have to start small, do that. And keep the bigger picture in your heart.

7. Continue to Speak Words of Faith

This caught my attention in this story:

> 6 Now it came to pass, when the vessels were full, that she said to her son, "Bring me another vessel."
> And he said to her, "There is not another vessel." So the oil ceased.

The moment the woman's son said there is not another vessel, and the woman accepted the message, the oil ceased. I don't know how many containers they filled before this time, but remember the prophet had said, borrow plenty vessels. I'm convinced that if they had run out of the house and hired more vessels, the oil would have continued to flow. They would have had more containers of oil, which would mean more money for the family. But no, the oil stopped flowing when they said, there are no more vessels.

What can we learn from that?

> *Your words are part of your healing and restoration process. What you say when you're going through challenges is very important. Your words can stop your progress or accelerate it.*

Be mindful of what you say during times of crisis. Don't speak like the world is over. Just because you don't immediately feel the manifestation of your words today does not mean that your words are nothing. They are secretly creating your next realities.

Don't stop your oil flow with your words. Speak faith no matter what's happening, and God will cause you to triumph.

8. Sell something

Elisha told the woman after all the prayers and prophetic declarations, ***"Go and sell the oil."***

Did the prayer work? Yes. Did the prophetic words produce? Yes. But she still had to go and sell the oil to raise the money she needed.

I can tell you that you've prayed a lot for financial breakthrough, God has heard your prayers. Now, go and sell something.

"Just like that, pastor?"

Yes, just like that.

When I came to Lagos in 2005, at the age of 28, I did not have any money to start any reasonable business. I wanted to learn computer, but I did not have money for the training. More so, where I was putting up, I had limited time to stay there.

The odds were stacked against me. I was the first son of my family. I had just relocated from the East where I had some leverage to a city where I didn't know anyone, except my uncle who I was living with. I believe I heard God telling me to relocate. And here I was in the city with no money, no contacts, no connections, and not many ideas.

I prayed. I fasted. But more importantly, I sat down and thought. I listened to my heart and was willing to do whatever it took to move forward.

Then it began to dawn on me: **you have to sell something.** The more you sell, the more money you'll make. The less you sell, the less money you'll make.

But there was a problem. I had nothing to sell (or so I felt). And even if I had something to sell, I had no money to buy those things to resell. And I had no one to borrow the money from. All this was enough to cause depression and lead me to anger toward God. But I thought, *"Hey. You have this cell phone. Why not sell it and use the money to go and buy some stuff and start selling."*

"Wow," I thought in my mind. *"I have something to start with after all."* And yes, everyone has something they can start with if they look well enough.

Eventually, I sold my Sagem phone that I came to Lagos with and went to Ojota and bought several easy topic pamphlets. The next day I went inside Molue (the big inner-city buses in Lagos), dressed very corporately (you would think I was working in one bank if you saw the way I dressed), and started hawking the books. I would stand up, greet the people, pray with them, share the Gospel, and afterward, sell the books.

I didn't know if it would succeed or not when I started, but I just wanted to sell something. Of course, there were a lot of things that put me off. Sometimes the bus drivers and their assistants (the conductors) would be so rude to me. Other times the passengers would be very unresponsive. But I moved on. That's the world we live in, a real world. People will be rude to you. People will be unresponsive many times. But you have to move on. Your life does not consist in what they do to you but in what you do with what God is putting in your heart.

From selling books inside buses, I found other things I could also sell. Despite all the obstacles, I pressed forward. Within six months, I had rented an office/house and moved out of my uncle's house. It wasn't easy, but it happened. And within three years (From 2005 to 2008), I had made my first million, (not in dollars please), bought my first car, and eventually got married traditionally in November 2009, and wedded in April 2010.

There are two things I've learned in life:

- ***With God all things are possible, and***
- ***Nothing is small when God is with you.***

Today, when I see young men and women who say they have no jobs and are gallivanting, looking for some financial assistance here and there, I know that they are not ready to dirty their hands. They are looking for some already made things, and some free money, which is always very hard to come by.

9. Stop Waiting and Start Selling

The way to get started is to get started. Don't wait to get all the details right. Start and things will start to get clearer as you go forward.

Stop waiting so long thinking of what to sell, expecting some strange ideas to fall on you. Make a list of things you usually spend money on almost all the time. Now select from one of those things, look for where to buy them in bulk and start reselling them. If you buy those things, people will buy them.

Elisha told the woman, "Go and sell…" I am telling you today by the Holy Spirit, "God has heard your prayers, now pick yourself up. Arise and start selling." Don't worry, none of those bad things you're afraid of will happen.

Yes, you will make mistakes, but its part of the game. I tried different kinds of network marketing in those years and many other different stuff that didn't work. I learned firsthand that while network marketing can be great, it's not always easy. ***The best way to start making money is to go and buy things and resell them***. Other things can be additional efforts to grow.

The internet has made it immensely easier today. There are many e-commerce sites where you can register for free and start selling stuff the next morning, even without having those things in your house. There are also websites where you can offer services and earn income.

I didn't say it will be easy. But that's the real world. Things are not easy in the real world. But the good news is that as you learn and practice, you'll grow and get better. And because God is with you, you will advance by the day.

10. Don't Be Afraid to Start Small

One of the biggest obstacles that people have in accessing financial breakthrough is their inability to accept small opportunities and open doors. Other times it is because opportunities come dressed as work.

I have seen people who are so bent on praying for one big money they are expecting to come that no matter what you say to them, they won't listen. They are bent on asking you to pray for God to cause that money they are expecting to come. They don't want to hear anything else. Unfortunately, they miss God's blessings with this stubbornness.

Stop carrying those contract papers and proposals up and down, anointing them and getting every man of God to pray over them. While you're expecting them to come, look out for small doors God is opening for you and start commanding your breakthrough through those open doors

God's blessings come in small packages. Accept the small entries he opens for you and be faithful in it. Those little openings will create big enterprises.

Every tree you see today started as a seed. And every seed has the potential of becoming a forest of trees. It all begins with planting the seed, watering it and taking care of it.

The Bible says:

> **He who is faithful in a very little thing is faithful also in much, and he who is unrighteous in a very little thing is unrighteous also in much.** - Luke 16:10

> Do not despise these small beginnings, for the Lord rejoices to see the work begin, to see the plumb line in Zerubbabel's hand." - Zechariah 4:10 (NLT)

The Lord enjoys seeing you start, for through your work he will answer your prayers.

What to Do Now

If you need an urgent financial breakthrough, then do this...

- Take responsibility for where you are right now
- Don't die in silence. Open up and ask for help
- Choose right over convenience
- Discern the oil in your house
- If you're going to borrow, only borrow for profit, not for survival
- Shut your door
- Continue to declare the word of faith
- Sell something.
- Stop waiting while praying, start selling while praying.
- Don't be afraid to start small

This will work because it's God's Word.

Action #4: **Ask the Right Questions**

"Ask, and it shall be given you; seek, and ye shall find; knock, and it shall be opened unto you: For every one that asketh receiveth; and he that seeketh findeth, and to him that knocketh it shall be opened." - Matthew 7:7-8

The book of Proverbs 26:2b says that *a curse without a cause will not come*. It's the same thing as saying that *every problem has a cause*. To put an end to a problem, we must identify the cause of the problem.

When you're going through a financial crisis, it's easy for you to feel so overcome that you don't get to assess the situation the way it is. But one thing is clear: ***feeling and acting emotional will not solve the problem.*** After all the tears and complains, you need to sit up and begin to ask yourself some critical questions.

What really happened? Why are you where you are today? How did it happen? What lessons can you learn from everything? Are there people who have gone through your kind of situation before? What did they do to get help? What can you do? What's your way forward right now?

> *"If you ask yourself the right questions and persist, you'll teach yourself much more in a day what others will spend five years learning in a school."*

It's not enough to say, "I need plenty of money now. I need one million. I want to pay this bill and have some freedom." And so on.

If you were to be given such money right now and you haven't identified what led to the financial crisis you're going through, you could still misuse the funds.

Almost every time, I have people saying to me, "Pastor, I need so and so amount of money to settle this matter right now. Please pray. I need an urgent miracle."

I always pray from my heart and support to the best of my ability. But I've found out that praying for and receiving financial miracles to solve urgent money problems (relating to bills) is like giving someone a fish when they are hungry. While the fish takes care of their immediate hunger problem, it doesn't stop them from getting hungry again.

So first things first. Ask yourself targeted questions and record your answers without any emotions. Find out what is responsible for where you are at the moment. Then take your observations to the Lord in prayer and ask for His mercy to make corrections where necessary. As I often say, God wants to give you more than your bills money. He wants to build you financially for His kingdom's sake.

What to Do Now

Always remember that no situation in life is entirely new. Many others have gone through what you are going through today and came through it. So push your imaginations far and take note of the answers to specific questions about where you are. Identify the causes of the problem, and you're halfway solving it.

Action #5: **Decrease Expenses and Increase Income**

"Lazy hands will make you poor; hard-working hands will make you rich." - Proverbs 10:4 (ERV)

We often don't need a prophecy to know that when income decrease and expenses increase, we will suffer financial hardship. It's as simple as ABC. And the funny thing about life is that expenses are always increasing. Most times it is income that is either always static or continuously decreasing.

It, therefore, makes a common sense to think of two things:

- How to increase income, and
- How to reduce expenses

Reducing expenses is a good idea, but it's not always easy. Sometimes even the necessary expenses can be so much that earned income is not ever enough to handle them. So experts recommend spending more effort thinking of how to increase income while trying to cut down on things that can be cut down.

Don't Ask for *'Bills Money,'* Pray for Business Money

God's purpose is not just to give you money to pay bills. On occasions, He sends us "bills money" through miraculous intervention, but His bigger plan is for us to be established that we won't need to cry each time there are bills to pay. So quit waiting and praying for bills money from time to time; start thinking and praying for business money.

There's nothing wrong with praying for bills money. Our merciful Father does supply all our needs according to His riches in glory. So when the bills are due, it doesn't hurt to ask in faith and believe for a miracle. But here's the thing:

> *You can't live your entire life always depending on miracles to pay your bills.*

Financial miracles do happen. I've seen it many times. But its purpose must not be mistaken. God sends us financial miracles as a way to give us relief from grave situations which do occur from time to time. But His ultimate purpose is for us to mature enough that we don't have to need such miracles any time bills come up. God wants us to have established means of income.

The Power of Multiple Streams of Income

There is a scripture that changed my life in 2016. It's Ecclesiastes 11:1-2. It says:

> 11 *Ship your grain across the sea; after many days you may receive a return.*
> 2 *Invest in seven ventures, yes, in eight; you do not know what disaster may come upon the land. (NIV)*

I've been reading this scripture for many years, but on that fateful day in 2016, I saw it in a different light.

First, it says to ship your grain across the sea. That's talking about international business, marketing your products globally.

As I thought about that, something clicked in my spirit: *The internet is God's tool for taking our products globally.* Unfortunately, we have either ignored it completely, ridiculed it, and left it for unbelievers, saying that there's so much evil there, or we just used it for social media gossip.

This insight inspired my online book publishing. I had to invest time to learn how to use the internet to distribute my books and other contents. This has led to thousands of lives changed globally and opened up a source of income for the ministry.

But secondly, and more stirring, the second verse says, **"invest in seven ventures, even in eight, for you do not know the disaster that may come on the land."**

As I looked at that verse, the Holy Spirit spoke to my heart and said, *"The only antidote to such disasters as economic crisis is multiple streams of income."* Without **a seven or eight venture mindset**, we'll always be caught up in the *disaster that may come upon the land*

That was the day my mindset changed. I understood and began to teach the importance of multiple streams of income. If we don't understand creating different streams of income, we may always be caught up in sudden bad financial policy changes, inflation, rising food costs, rising school fees, and other issues that will always lead to financial hardship.

> ***Without multiple streams of income, we may not experience lasting financial breakthrough.***

So step out today and begin to learn a couple of new things that can help you earn from more than one source of income. Start some side hustles even while focused on your present career. Learning to increase your income is vital to dealing with financial hardship and walking in financial breakthrough.

Wisdom

Your expenses are not likely to decrease soon. So while you're trying to cut some costs here and there, start learning to increase income.

Action #6: **Treat Debt Like a Plague**

Owe no one anything except to love one another, for he who loves another has fulfilled the law. - Romans 13:8

A plague is something that is causing continuous trouble, pain, distress, or irritation. Other words for plague are bane, curse, scourge, affliction, blight, cancer, canker, evil, etc. That is precisely what debt is. You must fight hard to deal with it.

I receive prayer requests daily from people wanting to have their debts canceled supernaturally, and those facing a lot of crisis due to debts. Plus my own experience as well. So I can tell you that debt is not a good thing. We must do everything we can to deal with living in debt.

While God can work miracles on your debt, it's easier to be free from debt by knowing what He says about it and obeying it. Not listening to God's words on debt can lead to God ignoring your prayers on debt and money, and there's nothing you can do to Him.

In 2 Kings 4, the prophet of God died from debt, and even when he died, his creditors still came to take his children to cover for his debt. We know that this man must have prayed and fasted for miraculous debt cancellation, but it didn't happen because God's full plan for his people is that they shouldn't live in debt in the first place.

There may be times that borrowing may seem justifiable, such as in health situation, but the majority of debts are not always that. Many times, debt is a consequence of our actions and poor business and financial decisions. Sometimes, too, it can be a result of forces outside our control.

> ***We live in a world system that encourages debt and borrowing. Sadly, this is against God's commandments on debt.***

To get out of debt, you have to start by reprogramming your mind. You have to start by convincing yourself that you can live without debt and borrowing; that you would better be a lender than a debtor.

The whole truth is that borrowing and debt are inviting tomorrow's evil today. We can choose to obey God and let each day carry its evil or continue to invite the burdens of the next day and the subsequent years on the present (Matthew 6:34).

God's Words on Debts

a. The debtor is a slave to the creditor: Debt invokes a slavery status on the debtor to the creditor (Proverbs 22:7). This isn't the position Christ wants us to be. He has paid all our debts and made us free. Forcing ourselves in debt is questioning His very work of redemption for us.

b. God wants us to lend to others instead: Sounds like a paradox, right? First, we say a borrower is a slave to the lender. Next, we say, God wants us to lend to others.

"For the Lord, your God will bless you just as He promised you; you shall lend to many nations, but you shall not borrow; you shall reign over many nations, but they shall not reign over you" (Deuteronomy 15:6, 28:12, Matthew 5:42).

The message is that if there's going to be anyone who will be a slave, then it shouldn't be the people in covenant with God. By being the lenders, we demonstrate that God is enough for us and does supply our needs. This way, we can attract the unbelievers to our God.

c. It is wickedness not to repay debts: - Psalm 37:21 says, *"The wicked borrows and does not repay, but the righteous shows mercy and gives."* And Romans 13:7 (MSG) reads: *"Fulfill your obligations as a citizen. Pay your taxes, pay your bills, and respect your leaders."*

Even though our legal system allows individuals and businesses in suffering to recuperate themselves under the protection of bankruptcy laws, as believers, we have a moral obligation to repay our creditors to the best of our ability. Applying the bankruptcy laws should only be in very critical situations.

This is also the same as praying for debt cancellation. You need to make efforts to repay your debts. You need to pray for a divine provision that will enable you to repay your debts. Only resort to praying for debt cancellation when the situation is very critical.

d. Don't be in haste to sign a guarantee for someone: *"Be sure you know a person well before you vouch for his credit! Better refuse than suffer later.*

Unless you have the extra cash on hand, don't countersign a note. Why risk everything you own? They'll even take your bed!" (Proverbs 11:15, 22:26-27 - TLB).

There's nothing to add there.

5. Be faithful in the little money you have: *He who is faithful in what is least is faithful also in much, and he who is unjust in what is least is unjust also in much. Therefore if you have not been faithful in the unrighteous mammon, who will commit to your trust the true riches?* (Luke 16:10-11)

6. Don't spend all your money on shopping: *The wise man saves for the future, but the foolish man spends whatever he gets* (Proverbs 21:20 - TLB).

7. Forgive debts owed you: if someone owing you money is unable to repay, and in all honesty, you can see that he is unable, the Bible says to forgive. Exercising forgiveness in such circumstances does not make you a fool. Instead by extending mercy, you obtain mercy in your matters as well (See Matthew 18:21-35 TLB).

8. Be content with what you have: *Stay away from the love of money; be satisfied with what you have. For*

God has said, 'I will never, never fail you nor forsake you' (Hebrews 13:5).

....

As you can see, while the Bible did not say that borrowing or debt is a sin, it does make it clear that it is not God's best for us. That is why the Apostle Paul counsels us in Romans 13:8 to *"owe no one anything except to love one another, for he who loves another has fulfilled the law."*

How to Be Free From Debt

There are times that the debts we find ourselves in are not of our own making. They could have been incurred as a result of things that were considered very urgent, or emergencies. However, there are other times that our debts are a result of our choices and mistakes. Whichever the case is, we can trust God completely for help and deliverance.

In the Scriptures, our sins are often treated as debts. When we genuinely repent and confess them to God, He forgives us and the process of complete restoration starts. The same can be done with our debts.

Step 1: Pray. List out all your debts in a paper and take them to the Lord in prayer. Take responsibility and ask for His mercy and forgiveness. Ask God for help with any habit or attitude that led you to those debts. Plead the Blood of Jesus Christ, and ask God for help with the debts.

> *Debt is a yoke and a weight that tries to keep us down. And God can give us rest from our yokes as we come to Him in faith through Christ Jesus (Matthew 11:28-29)*

Sometimes God's help with your debts may not necessarily be about canceling the debts, but about opening doors of new jobs for you so that you can earn more money to be able to pay your debts. Be open while you're praying and tell God you want a way out of those debts. Don't insist He must cancel the indebtedness because He already says you should pay back your debts.

While praying, commit yourself to stay with God's words on money and not the sophisticated financial system. God wants us to be the lenders and not the debtors. So stop borrowing. Stop going into more debts.

Step 2: Review and begin to deal with habits that lead to debts. Review your belief about debts and personal actions that keep you in debt. It starts with your mindset.

We have a rule in our home, which I learned from BishopDavid Oyedepo. The rule says: *If we can't afford it, then it's not yet the right time for it.*

Learn to start trusting God for your provisions and not your abilities. Often, we go into debts when we want things and lifestyles that we can't afford at the moment. We may believe that we desperately need those things and then go into debt. But the truth is that if we looked deeper, we didn't need them. There were alternatives (God's ways of escape) that we ignored.

If you can't afford a private school for your children today, send them to schools you can afford. Wear clothes you can afford; drive cars you can afford.

It is not wise to compare yourself with others and live a borrowed lifestyle.

Step 3: Don't run away from your debts. Don't try to cover the shame that the Lord has not covered. It will come back.

When our forex and investment business failed, and we ran into huge debts, our creditors dragged us to many different places. It wasn't easy. But thankfully, we never missed a meeting with them. Of course, there were all kinds of threats here and there. But we gently and prayerfully followed through with everything. When many of them saw that we didn't defraud them, they started to calm down and began to pray for us.

Yes, you can be praying for debt cancellation and pleading for God's intervention, but while you're doing that, don't try to act fraudulently by avoiding your creditors. Face your mess with confidence that God will make a way somehow.

Step 4: Recognize God's escape plans. The Bible says in 1 Corinthians 10:13 that *"No temptation has overtaken you except such as is common to man; but God is faithful, who will not allow you to be tempted beyond what you are able, but with the temptation will also make the way of escape, that you may be able to bear it."*

As you pray and seek God for help and deliverance from debt, He will make a way of escape. First, He will give you the grace to bear the pressures, and sustain your health.

Next, he will begin to open new doors for you: New business opportunities, new job offers, and new ideas. Don't get stuck with expecting miraculous debt cancellations or expecting that your creditors will forget that you owe them money that you fail to recognize and take advantage of God's escape plans. And as soon as you begin to see these new blessings, don't forget your debts.

Step 5: Employ the serpent skill. Jesus told us to be wise as a serpent but harmless as a dove. One area that the serpent is so good is in the area of negotiation. He negotiated Adam and Even out of the Garden of Eden, and even tried it with Christ, but failed.

As a further step to deal with your debt, negotiate with your creditors. Give them a call. Ask for a soft landing. Let them know you're doing your best. Demand forgiveness of some parts of the debt. Many will oblige when they see you honestly want to do something about the debt.

Step 6: Learn about money and investment God's way. All the suggestions I've outlined above are based on my experience and revelation. They should not replace professional financial counseling.

Wisdom

Read books on money and investment God's way, and learn Bible ways to approach finance. One thing I'm sure is that as you honestly pray and take divinely inspired steps towards your debts, God will make way for you.

Action #7: **The Miracle of 'Little Drops of Water'**

"The wise man saves for the future, but the foolish man spends whatever he gets." - Proverbs 21:20 (TLB)

Little drops of water can make a mighty ocean. That's an undeniable truth. You can try it yourself and see.

Treat the little monies you have in that light. They may be drops of water today, but they can add up to the ocean of finance you need in time to come.

There is this ad I always see on CNN. The business presenter is walking down the hallway, and a penny falls out from a woman's handbag. He picks it up and tells the woman, "This is yours." The woman looks up and says, "It's just a penny." Then the guy exclaims, "Just a Penny!"

Financial breakthrough begins with a penny. Use the pennies God provides for you wisely and your barn will increase with time.

Don't despise small monies.

The Wisdom of Savings

When I talk to people about savings, the most common excuse I get is, "I don't have enough." I remember someone saying to me some time ago, "Is it not when someone has enough that he will have to save?" As believable as that excuse may sound, it is not a credible reason not to save.

I know you may not want me to talk about savings since we're looking at how to deal with financial hardship and command financial breakthrough, and you may probably need some urgent breakthrough. But let's look at it this way: *if you had some savings, you may not have come to the point where you're now under pressure.*

A wise man thinks ahead; a fool doesn't and even brags about it!
(Proverbs 13:16 (TLB))

The idea of saving for the future is scriptural. It's part of God's wisdom for dealing with times of famine. In Genesis 41:34-36, Joseph recommended:

> 34 Let Pharaoh do this, and let him appoint officers over the land, to collect one-fifth of the produce of the land of Egypt in the seven

plentiful years. ₃₅ And let them gather all the food of those good years that are coming, and store up grain under the authority of Pharaoh, and let them keep food in the cities. ₃₆ Then that food shall be as a reserve for the land for the seven years of famine which shall be in the land of Egypt, that the land may not perish during the famine."

Without the wisdom of savings, Egypt would have been caught up in the famine. But with the knowledge and application of the savings key, they were spared.

Isn't that interesting?

No doubt, God had the power to do great miracles and cause the times of plenty in Egypt not to stop. But He didn't. He allowed the natural law of seasons and times to prevail.

Life is a product of seasons and times. There are always times of plenty and times of famine. It is what you do with your resources during times of plenty that determines the outcome of events during times of famine.

Jesus counseled that a man who wants to build a house should sit down and count the cost (Luke 14:28-30). He meant that we should sit down and draw plans for our lives. We should not leave our children's school fees, rent, accommodation, and other essential life issues to miracles. While miracles can and does happen, we should do our part first.

Saving is one of your required Biblical wisdom for lasting financial abundance. Without savings, you will not have what to invest with when an opportunity presents itself. Without savings, you will not have any immediate fall back plan when things change suddenly.

As a Christian, realize that we live in a real world, not a fantasy island. Don't use God and prayer as an excuse for laziness. Yes, God will bless you. He will protect you. He will provide for you. He will heal you. But you also need the wisdom to play your part. There are things required of you. And when it comes to money and financial breakthrough, *savings is one of God's ideas for keeping you blessed.*

How do I save? Where do I save? How can I get the best returns on savings? Etc.

I'll leave you to find the answers to all of those questions in other practical finance books. But here are a few savings tips to get started.

General Savings Tips

- Start now, don't wait for a perfect time.
- Start small. Little drops of water can fill an ocean.
- Open an emergency account.
- Make budgets for each month
- Take note of all your expenditures for the month. This will help you see where you can cut down costs and where your money is going.
- Don't just save money that you will withdraw as soon as one thing comes up. Tie each of your savings to a project – college for children, house, landed property, rent, car, etc.
- Save automatically. Discuss with your bank or sign up with some modern day savings institutions to automatically withdraw a specific amount from your income and pool it into your savings pot.
- Let your money work for you. Don't just save money by leaving it in the bank. That is not savings. Put money in financial products that yields

some interest after some time, no matter how small.

- Invest in property. Open an account with a real estate company and start paying for a property using a flexible plan. It may take time but remember the law of little drops of water.

- When you have some windfall – unexpected financial blessings – after giving to God, save some from it. Don't spend all on shopping.

- Download some savings app that can give you a savings reminder.

- Buy things in bulk. It helps you save some money through discounts

- Attend financial classes and get some free financial advise

- Don't wait for things to get bad before you do some health checkups. Prevention is cheaper in the long run than cure.

- Always compare alternatives before any major purchase. You'll get some discounts most times

I keep these tips handy to remind me of God's wisdom to save. I'm not a full-blown accountant, and this is not an all-out finance management book. So while the tips here can help you, I recommend that you get some further education on the different savings opportunity you can find in the country you live, your state and your banks.

Action #8: **Scale Forward**

But the path of the just is like the light of dawn, that shines brighter and brighter until [it reaches its full strength and glory in] the perfect day. - Proverbs 4:18 (AMP)

God wants your today to be better than your yesterday, and your tomorrow to be better than your today. That is from glory to glory living. Anything short of that is not His will for your life.

Many people get to a point in their lives that they become stagnant, and are not going forward or backward. They become so used to their routine that it becomes difficult for them to move out of their cocoon. They become so used to their jobs, their shops, and their present endeavors. They find it very difficult to move beyond where they are.

I believe in starting small, but I don't believe in remaining small. I believe in moving forward.

I started in Lagos selling inside Molue buses. But I moved on with time. At a stage I started doing training, investing in other businesses, and learning other skills. Sadly, there are people I met selling in the buses in those years that are still there many years after.

> **"When we were at Mount Sinai, the LORD our God said to us, 'You have stayed at this mountain long enough** - Deut 1:6 (NLT)

Look at that. Mount Sinai is also known as Mount Horeb, or the Mount of God. They were there waiting on the Lord, then God came and said, "You've stayed long on this mountain. It's time to go forward.

That's like saying, *"Hey, you've prayed and fasted long enough. It's time to break camp and move forward."*

Praying and fasting and waiting on the Lord are great spiritual exercises every Christian must do from time to time. But there's time to break camp and go forward. There's time to act. It is in the going forward that you prove the power of God's promises.

Growth And Expansion Are God's Plan

As a salary earner, your income and financial breakthrough are dependent on the goodness of your boss. That's very straightforward. So, if you're not okay with your present take home, do something about it. And other than just pray, start some side businesses, learn new skills, expand.

As a shop owner, look for other things to add, subtract, and multiply. If your present wares are not selling enough, no one says you should die there. Be open to change and advancement. Never come to a point in your life that you're now comfortable with the status quo.

I said some time ago, "if you're currently worth 5 Million, don't be stuck there. God is testing you. He wants you to be worth 50 million." Yield to him in humility and let him take you where He wants you.

I feel the Lord is speaking to you right now.

> *"You have stayed long enough where you are. It's time to move out of your comfort zone and advance."*

You'll never really know the magnitude of what you can achieve until you begin to desire increase and work towards it with practical actions.

Action #9: A Forgotten Lesson from the Widow of Zarephath

"These things I have spoken to you while being present with you. But the Helper, the Holy Spirit, whom the Father will send in My name, He will teach you all things, and bring to your remembrance all things that I said to you." - John 14:25-26

When you hear the widow of Zarephath, what quickly comes to your mind?

For many, it's how the woman gave her last meal and never had to lack because God continued to multiply her bread miraculously. The narrative fits in many times when we are charging people to give. Let's read the story before we proceed

> ₇Sometime later the brook dried up because there had been no rain in the land. ₈Then the word of the Lord came to him: ₉*"Go at once to Zarephath in the region of Sidon and stay there.*

I have directed a widow there to supply you with food."

¹⁰So he went to Zarephath. When he came to the town gate, a widow was there gathering sticks. He called to her and asked, "Would you bring me a little water in a jar so I may have a drink?" ¹¹As she was going to get it, he called, "And bring me, please, a piece of bread."

¹²"As surely as the Lord your God lives," she replied, *"I don't have any bread—only a handful of flour in a jar and little olive oil in a jug. I am gathering a few sticks to take home and make a meal for myself and my son, that we may eat it—and die."*

¹³Elijah said to her, *"Don't be afraid. Go home and do as you have said. But first, make a small loaf of bread for me from what you have and bring it to me, and then make something for yourself and your son. ¹⁴For this is what the Lord, the God of Israel, says:* **'The jar of flour will not be used up, and the jug of oil will not run dry until the day the Lord sends rain on the land.'"**

¹⁵She went away and did as Elijah had told her. So there was food every day for Elijah and for the woman and her family. ¹⁶For the jar of flour

was not used up and the jug of oil did not run dry, in keeping with the word of the Lord spoken by Elijah. **- 1 Kings 17:7-16**

While we can learn the power of exercising faith in God and giving even when things are hard for us, there's the other lesson in this story that you must learn and apply in your life.

First, God spoke to Elijah and told him to leave the brook. Then He told him where to go and what widow to meet, including what to say to the widow.

That's the main key to the miracle: i.e., the *Divine instruction obeyed*.

> ***It is not the giving that provoked the miracle, but the instruction from God that was obeyed.***

That's the lesson that we often miss out from the story.

Instruction is more important than giving. You may give and give and give, but if you are disregarding God's instructions in your heart, you may not experience any breakthrough. It is God's instruction obeyed that triggers the miraculous.

If after reading this scripture, for example, I call one widow in the church and say, *"Look at that. Go and bring me all the food items in your house. God's gonna multiply the left over."* The woman may do that, but there would be no supernatural growing of her food because I acted on my own. I was not instructed.

Unfortunately, that's what happens in the Church today. Preachers concoct a lot of things and push people to give, assuring them that they will experience a supernatural breakthrough. Sometimes they even give people timeframes to expect this breakthrough - ten days, seven days, thirty days, etc. Sadly, nothing changes after everything.

As preachers, let us make it a duty to be instructed before we start charging people with this scripture to give. When God instructs to collect the offering, the act of obedience of the people will bear fruit. Divinely commanded or instructed giving will provoke supernatural breakthroughs. But human-made manipulations will not work because we cannot manipulate God.

Here's the balance we must recreate...

- Give because the Word of God has already told us to give.

- When there's a call for a special offering or seeds in the church, give because it is God's will to support the church and the cause of the Gospel.

- The Bible instructs us to give. It teaches us to support the church, plant into the gospel, give to the poor, GIVE TO MINISTRIES, give to our parents, and others.

- ***But our giving must be done out of love for God and desire to support good causes, not with a mindset that we will bribe God enough to bless us financially.***

God's blessings do not flow down to us according to our numerous works, but according to His mercy and our obedience to His instruction. This means three things:

1. He will bless you because He has said so and He is faithful to His words. His mercy will make it happen.

2. You will give because you love him. Not because you want to move him with your giving. He owns

everything. You do not have anything that does not already belong to Him.

3. More importantly, as you serve Him, you will continue to strive to hear His instructions to you per time and endeavor to obey. Your obedience will cause you to eat the good of the land

Pray This Prayer

Dear Heavenly Father,

I ask for forgiveness today regarding my wrong alignment and faulty belief about giving. How often do I give with a wrong mindset. Today, Lord, I understand and accept that everything I have comes from You and belongs to You. I am not giving to buy You over but to honor and serve you.

From this day, Lord, continually remind me by Your Spirit that your instruction is more important than all sacrifices, for in my obedience I demonstrate my faith in Your power.

In Jesus name, I pray.

What to Do Now

Giving is very vital in our service to God because it is a way to deal with greed. While greed says *"accumulate all, and more for yourself, you don't have enough yet, so keep all of it,"* God says, *"share with your neighbor; support a genuine course; support the church; start with what you have."*

However, our giving must be done from a mindset of love for God and a desire to support good causes. Not from the mindset that we can move God with what we have given to send money to us. There's nothing we have that doesn't belong to God. His financial blessings are not because we gave an offering, but because He has promised to provide for us.

Action #10: **Divine Instructions Will Bring Breakthrough**

"If you will only let me help you, if you will only obey, then I will make you rich! But if you keep on turning your backs and refusing to listen to me, you will be killed by your enemies; I, the Lord, have spoken." - Isaiah 1:19-20 (TLB)

The New Living Translation renders that passage this way: *"If you only obey me, you will have plenty to eat. But if you turn away and refuse to listen, you will be devoured by the sword of your enemies. I, the Lord, have spoken!"*

Look at that. It didn't say if you will bring plenty of offerings, but if you will obey.

The sword of the enemies rendered here does not mean war or death. It also implies scarcity, disappointments, frustrations, and financial lack. Wherever these things abound, if you look very deeply, there is some level of disobedience in place.

The biggest need of the present day Christian is learning when God is speaking to their hearts, confirming God's leading, and doing what He is telling them to do. No demon can stop Christians when they align their lives this way. The constant running up and down in frustration that has overtaken the church today will cease by simple acts of obedience.

"You can't give your away out of poverty while living in disobedience."

Let me share with you a story I heard from Rev. Nwandu, Senior pastor, Tower of Praise International, to shade some light on the power of discerning God's instructions and voice to you and following it. A sister was in a dream and was instructed to go and share the Gospel with a man down the street where she was staying. She subsequently obeyed. The first day, she went and shared the gospel with the man. A few days later, she went again and preached to the man. Then, she went a third time and preached to this same man.

On the third visit, the man requested for a prayer of protection for the journey he was about to embark. After the prayers he said to the sister, "Do you have anyone looking for a job, I might be able to help." The sister replied, "Oh, my two boys. They have finished their youth service and have been searching for a job." The man replied, "Ok, send me their CV."

Weeks later, the man helped this two job seekers secure a job in a multinational company.

No doubt, this was a big breakthrough. But as you can see, this breakthrough is not a result of offerings or seeds of faith. It came on the heels of God's instruction obeyed.

Prayerfully Listen to God's New Ideas

When people are going through financial problems, they may be so consumed with the issues they are going through that they don't listen to God's new ideas in their hearts. But if you go through scriptures, God usually answers prayers for a financial breakthrough by telling people what to do, not by throwing money down from the sky.

You can check out the following examples:

a. Peter (Luke 5:1-8)
b. The widow (2Kings 4:1-7)

c. Isaac (Genesis 26: 1-14)

Let me say this here: *"**God will not necessarily throw money down from the sky as an answer to your prayers for financial breakthrough. He may not tell anyone to call you and send you money.**"*

It's wrong to insist that God will talk to people to call you and give you money. You may have heard that kind of testimony from time to time, but that's not how God works and answers prayers for financial breakthrough. Those are rare and occasional situations. You cannot live your life hoping on them.

There was a time I was in a terrible financial problem. I desperately needed money to pay rent. I prayed and prayed and expected God to do some miracle per se. I cried and prayed all night. But nothing happened. Things got worse as the weeks turned into months. I thought God was not answering my prayers.

But it was in that season that God gave me a new business idea. Yes, that idea did not bring immediate finances, but as I began to work on it, many lives have been blessed from that single business. That business has helped hundreds of others put food on their table.

You may hear preachers share testimonies of how God talked to someone and then the person called them and sent them money that solved their financial problems. Don't get annoyed with God if things don't happen to you like that. Most times, that is how God blesses ministers: by using others to bless them. But the generality of His children, He blesses them other ways – through the works of their hands and by instructing them in their hearts what to do. This does not mean that He loves the preachers more. He loves all us the same and wants to provide for us.

Pray This Prayer

Dear Holy Spirit, teach me what I do not know about financial prosperity. Show me things hidden from men and bring unto my remembrance things You have spoken to me in the past that I ignored. Guide me in the way that I should go even as I desire and pray for breakthrough this day, in Jesus name.

What to Do Now

When you are earnestly praying for a financial breakthrough, watch it and pay attention. God will answer your prayers by giving you new ideas and opening new doors. You may not have a dream or hear an audible voice, but yes, God will guide you. Prayerfully discern what God is revealing to you and follow His leading.

GOD

BLESS

YOU

Get in Touch

We love testimonies.

We love to hear what God is doing around the world as people draw close to Him in prayer. If this book has blessed...

Please share your story with us.

Also, please consider giving this book a review on Amazon and checking out our other titles at:

amazon.com/author/danielokpara

Kindly do check out our website at www.BetterLifeWorld.org, and send us your prayer request. As we join faith with you, God's power will be made manifest in your life.

Other Books by the Same Author

---

1. <u>Prayer Retreat:</u> 21 Days Devotional With Over 500 Prayers & Declarations to Destroy Stubborn Demonic Problems.

2. <u>HEALING PRAYERS & CONFESSIONS</u>

3. <u>200 Violent Prayers</u> for Deliverance, Healing, and Financial Breakthrough.

4. <u>Hearing God's Voice in Painful Moments</u>

5. <u>Healing Prayers:</u> Prophetic Prayers that Brings Healing

6. <u>Healing WORDS:</u>   Daily Confessions & Declarations to Activate Your Healing.

7. <u>Prayers That Break Curses</u> and Spells and Release Favors and Breakthroughs.

8. <u>120 Powerful Night Prayers</u> That Will Change Your Life Forever.

9. <u>How to Pray for Your Children Everyday</u>

10. <u>How to Pray for Your Family</u>

11. <u>Daily Prayer Guide</u>

12. <u>Make Him Respect You:</u> 31 Very Important Relationship Intelligence for Women to Make their Men Respect them.

13. <u>How to Cast Out Demons from Your Home, Office & Property</u>

14. <u>Praying Through the Book of Psalms</u>

15. <u>The Students' Prayer Book</u>

16. <u>How to Pray and Receive Financial Miracle</u>

17. <u>Powerful Prayers to Destroy Witchcraft Attacks</u>.

18. <u>Deliverance from Marine Spirits</u>

19. <u>Deliverance From Python Spirit</u>

20. <u>Anger Management God's Way</u>

21. <u>How God Speaks to You</u>

22. <u>Deliverance of the Mind</u>

23. <u>20 Commonly Asked Questions About Demons</u>

24. <u>Praying the Promises of God</u>

25. <u>When God Is Silent</u>! What to Do When Prayer Seems Unanswered or Delayed

26. <u>I SHALL NOT DIE</u>: Prayers to Overcome the Spirit and Fear of Death.

27. Praise Warfare

28. Prayers to Find a Godly Spouse

29. How to Exercise Authority Over Sickness

30. Under His Shadow: Praying the Promises of God for Protection (Book 2).

31. 31 Days With Jesus: 5 Minutes Daily Meditations and Prayers to Learn More of Jesus, Connect More With Him, and Be More Like Him

About the Author

Daniel Chika Okpara is an influential voice in contemporary Christian ministry. His mandate is to make lives better through the teaching and preaching of God's Word with signs and wonders.

He is the senior pastor of Shining Light Christian Center, Lagos, Nigeria, a fast growing Church where God's word is the

pillar of everything. A foremost Christian teacher and author whose books are in high demand in prayer groups, Bible studies, and for personal devotions, he has authored over 50 life-transforming books and manuals on business, prayer, relationship and victorious living, many of which have become international best-sellers.

He is the president and CEO of Better Life World Outreach Center, a non-denominational ministry dedicated to global evangelism, prayer revival and empowering of God's people with the WORD to make their lives better. He is also the founder of Breakthrough Prayers Foundation (www.breakthroughprayers.org), an online portal leading people all over the world to encounter God and change their lives through prayer. Every day, thousands of people use the Breakthrough Prayers Portal to pray, and hundreds of testimonies from all around the world are received through it.

He is a Computer Engineer by training and holds a Master's Degree in Christian Education from Cornerstone Christian University. He is married to Doris Okpara, his best friend, and the most significant support in his life. They are blessed with lovely   children.

WEBSITE: www.betterlifeworld.org

NOTES